Stripes

By Miriam Frost
Illustrated by Cindy Clark

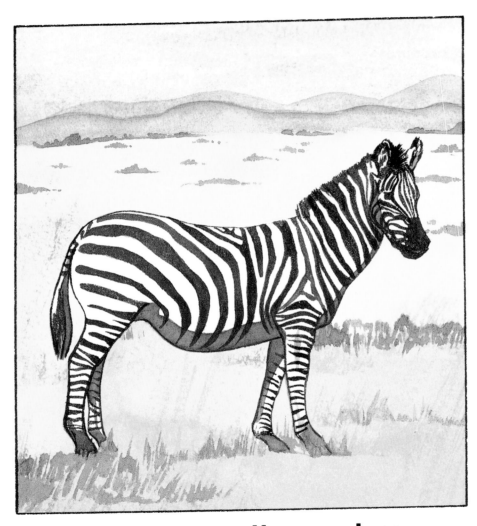

Stripes on the zebra.

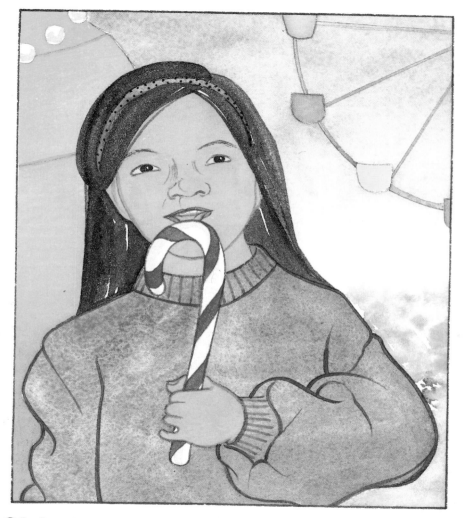

Stripes on the candy cane.

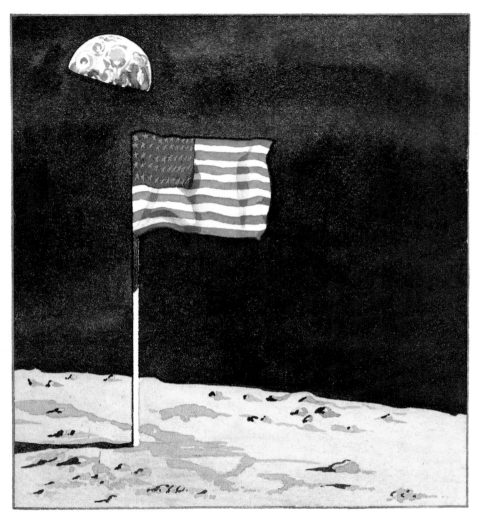

Stripes on the flag.

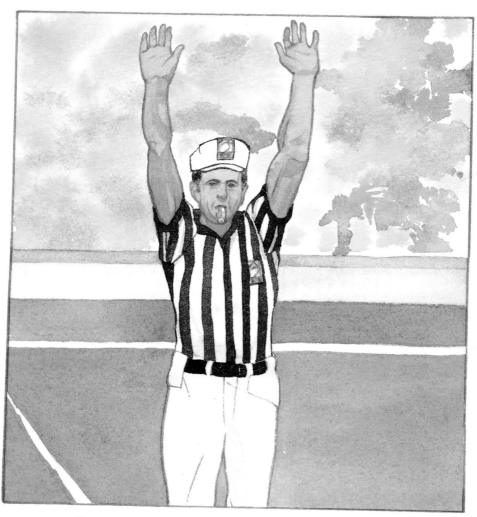

Stripes on the shirt.

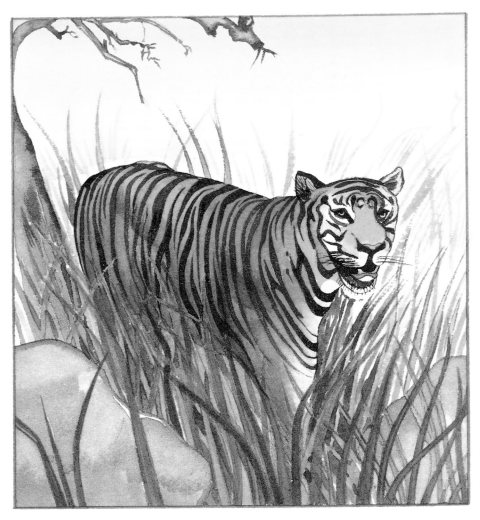

Stripes on the tiger.

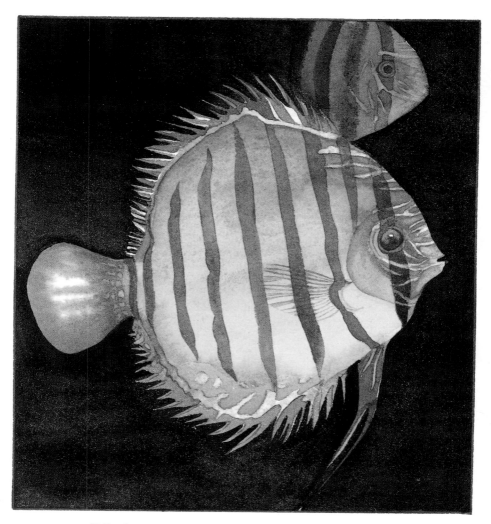

Stripes on the fish.

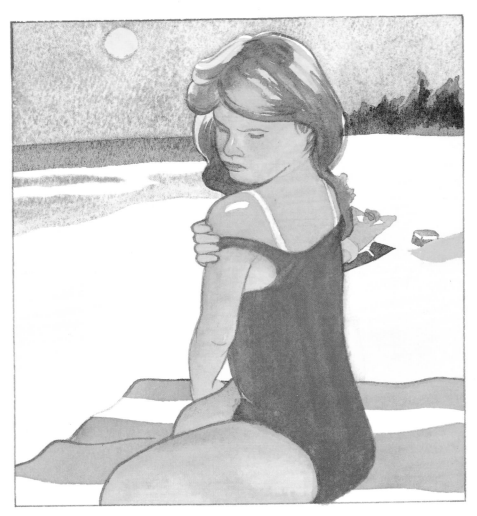

Stripes on me!